YOUR ROLES AND RESPONSIBILITIES AS A BOARD MEMBER

John Carver and Miriam Mayhew Carver

Jossey-Bass Publishers
San Francisco

Copyright © 1996 by Jossey-Bass Inc., Publishers, 350 Sansome Street, San Francisco, California 94104.

Jossey-Bass is a registered trademark of Jossey-Bass Inc., A Wiley Company.

No part of this publication may be reproduced, stored in a retrieval system, or transmitted in any form or by any means, electronic, mechanical, photocopying, recording, scanning, or otherwise, except as permitted under Sections 107 or 108 of the 1976 United States Copyright Act, without either the prior written permission of the Publisher or authorization through payment of the appropriate per-copy fee to the Copyright Clearance Center, 222 Rosewood Drive, Danvers, MA 01923, (978) 750-8400, fax (978) 750-4744. Requests to the Publisher for permission should be addressed to the Permissions Department, John Wiley & Sons, Inc., 605 Third Avenue, New York, NY 10158-0012, (212) 850-6011, fax (212) 850-6008, e-mail: permreq@wiley.com.

Manufactured in the United States of America.

Adapted from *A New Vision of Board Leadership: Governing the Community College*, by John Carver and Miriam Mayhew, Association of Community College Trustees, Washington, DC, 1994, and *Boards That Make a Difference*, Jossey-Bass, 1990.

Policy Governance℠ is a service mark of John Carver.

Library of Congress Cataloging-in-Publication Data

Carver, John.
    Your roles and responsibilities as a board member / John Carver and Miriam Mayhew Carver.
        p. cm. — (The CarverGuide series on effective board governance ; 2)
        ISBN 0-7879-0297-7 (pbk.)
        1. Directors of corporations. 2. Corporate governance.
I. Carver, Miriam Mayhew. II. Title. III. Series: Carver, John. CarverGuide series on effective board governance ; 2.
HD2745.C374 1996
658.4'22—dc20   96-10045

PB Printing   10 9 8 7 6 5   FIRST EDITION

Board members can be successful strategic leaders if they nurture their sense of group responsibility. All members must participate in the discipline and productivity of the group. All members must be willing to challenge and urge each other on to big dreams, lucid values, and fidelity to their trusteeship. All members must cherish diversity in viewpoints as well as the challenge of reaching an unambiguous, single board position derived from that diversity. All members must strive for accountability in the board's job, confident that if quality dwells in the boardroom, the rest of the organization will take care of itself.

Each board member carries important individual responsibilities in this pursuit of quality. These responsibilities are often written as a job description for board members. In this CarverGuide, we will describe the essentials of the board member's job, as determined by the Policy Governance model. But first, to make the job fully understandable, we must examine the board's governance process.

The Governance Process

Board members, not staff, are morally trustees for the ownership and, consequently, must bear initial responsibility for the integrity of governance. A board's relationship to those who, in a moral if not legal sense, own the organization is its primary relationship—far outweighing the board's relationship to its CEO and staff. It is out of the board's obligation to act on the behalf of this larger group that the board's job springs.

Hence, the point of departure for defining the board's job is in terms of making sure something happens on behalf of the ownership, not in terms of what the board does about internal organizational matters. For example, the board does not exist to help the staff, but to stand in for the owners. The board does not exist to supply auxiliary skills to the staff.

Board members can help staff, of course, but it is crucial to remember that such help is not why the board exists; that is, helping staff is not the purpose of governance. Such help to staff should be by board members as individual volunteers in order to make use of board members' valuable aid without compromising the integrity of governance.

The board's proper exercise of owners' authority is the beginning of accountability. The board cannot escape its personal responsibility for its own development, its own job design, its own discipline, and its own performance. Primary responsibility for board development does not rest in the chief executive, staff, funding bodies, or government.

It is inviting to rely on the chief executive to provide motivation for a board. This scenario frequently extends further than the provision of an occasional motivation "fix." It often extends as far as spoonfeeding. No matter how well the executive tells the board what to do and when to do it, governance cannot be excellent under these conditions. Going through the motions, even the "right" motions, is fake leadership that transforms a chief executive into a baby-sitter. Only a deluded board waits for its CEO to make it a good board.

As a board sets out to fulfill its trusteeship, its most immediate responsibility is to deal with the implications of being a group. Indeed, this hurdle can easily keep a board from attending to other responsibilities. Boards are fraught with extensive interpersonal dynamics as is any other group of human beings. We want to persuade the reader that taking time to design a sound governance process, before the process becomes personalized, is the greatest safeguard against the debilitating effects of unfortunate interpersonal dynamics. A sound design of the board's job will assure good governance even more than picking board members who are perfectly intelligent, communicative, assertive, and mentally healthy! In other words, you cannot overcome bad design with good people.

Carefully designing areas of board job performance will profoundly channel the interpersonal process of a board. For example, job design influences the types of conflict that will be experienced and whether members will follow a commonly proclaimed discipline or their individual disciplines. Diversity is directed toward some areas and muted or eliminated in others. Clarifying tasks and off-limits topics helps to depersonalize subsequent struggles when different individuals have opposing views about the appropriateness of an issue for board discussion.

A sound, codified governance process can ameliorate jockeying for power, control of the group through negativism, and diversion of the board into unrelated topics. One way in which the board participates in good process is by establishing explicit policies concerning the topic in the governance process category. The chairperson can then preserve the process by referring to board policy, which is easier and more legitimate than invoking disciplinary measures on the basis of his or her individual sense of what should be. Board members expect too much of the chairperson, for example, when they ask him or her to save the board from being held hostage by its most controlling member. Each member has the right to want to run things or never to budge. But, as a body, the board does not have the right to allow these individual proclivities to destroy the process.

Though the chairperson bears particular responsibility with respect to governance process, the entire board cannot avoid its share of responsibility. In other words, the existence of a chairperson does not relieve other board members from contributing to the integrity of the process. If the board as a whole does not accept responsibility for the governance process, the best the chairperson can achieve is superficial discipline. Moreover, board discipline achieved by virtue of the chairperson alone can easily be lost when the office turns over.

Construction of governance process policies begins with consideration of the board's overall reason for existence, because the ultimate test of process is whether this reason is fulfilled. So the board's "megaproduct" is the bridge that translates between those to whom the board is accountable and those who are accountable to the board.

Developing an effective governance process begins with clarification of the specific contributions of this bridge between owners and producers. Before we can intelligently design a governance process, we must be sure of what the board exists to accomplish: "form follows function." Appropriate practices are determined on the basis of the accomplishments expected. The board job description is thus the central factor in the governance process.

The Basic Board Job Description

Unfortunately, almost all published definitions of the board's job are statements of activities or methods: approve budgets, make policy, oversee finances, participate in discussion, hire the CEO, read monitoring reports, listen to input, review plans, read the mailings, learn to read financial statements, become better communicators, attend meetings, keep minutes, call on donors, and so on ad infinitum. It is not that these oft-prescribed engagements are wrong, but using activities as the beginning point for describing the board's job actually sabotages board leadership. It is possible for boards to carry out all the activities prescribed by the conventional wisdom and still fail to fulfill a useful organizational role.

Policy Governance requires the board's job, just like the CEO's job, to be described by its "values added," or, if you will, job products, rather than by its types of busy-ness. How is the organization different because this job exists? What does this job contribute? In describing job contributions, we speak of job "products" simply to keep before us at all times the output aspect of work rather than the activity aspect.

A governing board can make any number of contributions to its organization. But the choice of those board outputs should not be merely a laundry list of board member interests. Nor will responsible board leadership be achieved by accepting by rote the usual list of board activities handed down by traditional practice. We must craft a more effective blueprint than either chance or conventional wisdom can give us. Let us introduce our own definitions of responsibility and accountability in order to address this need for a blueprint.

No one argues against individuals taking responsibility for their individual actions. José is responsible for his contributions to the organization. Sally is responsible for hers, and so on. But suppose José and Sally work under the supervision of Maria. Maria, just like any other individual, is responsible for her contributions to the organization. Yet Maria is responsible for the work output of José and Sally as well as her own. That extra burden went along with Maria's accepting the job of supervisor.

Let's say that Maria and some others at her level report directly to the CEO, Jill. Jill is responsible for her own contributions to the total just like everyone else. Yet Jill is also responsible for the output of the entire organization of workers. At each level of organization, a worker bears what we might call simple responsibility for his or her own behavior but also bears a cumulative responsibility for all workers under his or her purview. At each level of management, the manager needs to be very aware of his or her cumulative responsibility—for that is the total output that his or her supervisor is looking at. In other words, a manager is responsible for producing something himself or herself, but the greater importance is the production of the entire organization part over which he or she has been given authority.

"Big Picture" water level rises – everyone is affected.

We will refer to the simple, direct responsibility for one's own work as "responsibility." We will refer to the bottom-up accumulation of responsibility for others' work together with one's own as "accountability." We realize that other definitions can be given to these words, but whatever words are used, we definitely need to distinguish between these two concepts.

In this way, it can be seen that the board has "accountability" for the entire organizational behavior—often referred to in normal discourse as "ultimate accountability." But the board's own job within that undoably large challenge—its "responsibility"—must be designed very carefully. The aim is to construe the board's responsibility (its job description) so that if it is carried out acceptably, the board's accountability is fulfilled.

Another way of stating this is that most of what a board is accountable for is out of reach, too complex and expansive for the board to touch directly. Most organizational decisions, for example, are "hands-off" matter for the board by necessity even if not by choice. But the responsibility of the board is the doable, "hands-on" piece of the total from which we must design board meetings, seek "matches" and skills in recruiting new members, and thus differentiate the board's job from everyone else's.

Whatever a board delegates to its CEO, then, is removed from the board's own responsibility, though clearly it remains accountable for it. By sheer necessity, most decisions in an organization are delegated away from the board. Indeed, because the board's leadership is so critical, it is best to delegate everything that can be delegated in order not to dilute the few unique contributions that can be made only by the board. Only three products cannot be delegated by a board. These form an irreducible trio applicable to all governing bodies, a short list but constructed so that the board's accountability for the total is not circumvented in the name of simplicity.

If accomplished, these direct job responsibilities of the board ensure the board's overall accountability as well. Thus, differentiating between the "hands-on" and "hands-off" aspects of the board's obligation saves the board from acting as if everything is its job. Let me summarize the job products of the board:

1. *The board's first direct product is the organization's linkage to the ownership.* The board acts in trusteeship for "ownership" and serves as the legitimizing connection between this base and the organization.
2. *The board's second direct product is explicit governing policies.* The board has the obligation to fulfill fiduciary responsibility, guard against undue risk, determine program priorities, and

generally direct organization activity. A board can be accountable yet not directly responsible for these obligations by setting the policies that will guide them. The values and perspectives of the whole organization can be encompassed by the board's explicit enunciation of broad policies if those policies follow a few simple principles.

3. *The board's third direct product is assurance of executive performance.* The board is obliged to ensure that the staff faithfully serves the board's policies. If the CEO continually fails to fulfill these explicit expectations, the board is itself culpable. The board has no choice but to take the steps necessary to remedy the situation. Although the board is not responsible for the performance of staff, it must ensure that staff (as a whole, not individually) meet the criteria the board has set. In this way, its accountability for that performance is fulfilled.

These three undelegable job contributions are the unique responsibilities of a governing board—unique because only the governing body can contribute these products. The board may add other products to this list, but it cannot shorten it and still responsibly govern.

You will notice that the board's job outputs are always means as opposed to ends. (Ends, remember, are direct statements of what consumer results are to be achieved, for which consumer groupings, and at what worth.) This should not be surprising inasmuch as the organization does not exist to have good governance. Good governance exists to describe and assure a good organization. While it is the staff's job to create the outputs of a good organizational performance, it is the board's job to define them.

Exhibit 1 depicts a policy drafted at one time by the board of the United States Cycling Federation (USCF), subsequently renamed USA Cycling, Inc. (USACI), a membership organization located in Colorado Springs. Remember that this policy describes the board's job, not the organization's job. Of all the "gifts" that it takes to make an organization work, which ones does the board contribute? That is, in addition to staff contributions, what does the board bring to the party?

> **Exhibit 1. Board Policy of the United States Cycling Federation (USCF).**
>
> *Policy Type:* Governance Process
> *Policy Title:* Board Job Description
>
> The job of the board is to make contributions that lead USCF toward the desired performance and assure that it occurs.
>
> The obligations of the board shall be
>
> 1. The link between USCF and its membership.
> 2. Written governing policies that, at the broadest level, address
>   A. Ends: products of the federation, impacts, benefits, outcomes. What good will the federation do for whose needs and at what cost?
>   B. Executive limitations: prudence and ethics boundaries for executive authority, activity, and decisions.
>   C. Governance process: specifications of how the board conceives, carries out, and monitors its task.
>   D. Board-executive director relationship: how power is delegated and its proper use monitored.
> 3. The assurance of executive director performance.
>
> ---
>
> *Source:* Reprinted with the permission of USA Cycling.

The USCF board determined that the board's job purpose, most broadly stated, is to make whatever "contributions . . . lead . . . toward the desired performance and assure" that performance. While the preamble only gives a broad-brush explication of the job outputs of the board, the finer points 1–3 make the outputs far clearer.

The first point in Exhibit 1 obligates the board to produce a link between the thousands of members of USCF and the operating organization. This board recognizes that it is the "bridge" between those who own USCF (its members) and the organization they own.

Annually, the board might further define what level of thoroughness or inclusiveness is to be achieved in this linkage. That is, the board might be more definitive about the nature of that linkage. In some year to come, for example, the USCF board (now USACI) might expand the wording to say that linkage will mean that 20 percent of the membership will participate in focus groups or surveys about what they think their federation should produce for them. In the service of this linkage, the board will devise activities, such as meeting with regional representatives, having more membership access to board members during annual conventions, or other methods of producing a more effective linkage.

The board's second point states that the board policies themselves are an important job contribution of the board. The policies must cover the four categories listed. For the staff to manage well, the board must govern well, and governing well involves converting the sundry opinions and values of individual board members into a consistent set of explicit values and positions.

USACI's third point connects board performance to CEO performance. If the CEO does not perform acceptably (as measured against the policies created in 2A and 2B), the board is therefore not performing acceptably. The board's job description not only pays homage to the board's accountability for staff effectiveness but also clearly states that if the CEO doesn't get the job done, the board cannot score well in subsequent evaluation of its own achievement.

Optional Board Products

Although all other contributions to the organization beyond the core three may be delegated to the CEO, it does not necessarily follow that the board should delegate them. One of the most common additional board products involves fund-raising.

Should a board be responsible for fund-raising? The answer depends on the kind of organization and its circumstances. From the perspective of governance concepts per se, one can only say that fund-raising, at the board's discretion, may be either delegated or retained. If a board chooses to assume this responsibility, it should define the contribution well enough that there is no confusion between staff and board responsibilities. One possible source of confusion is that "fund-raising" is an activity, not a result. Using results language will more likely force the board to confront the task it has taken on and its expectations of staff. For example, does the board merely make philanthropic contacts and leave responsibility for actually bringing in the money to staff? Or is the board responsible for the funding level, that is, everything up to and including the goal amount? Or does its responsibility lie somewhere in between? Wasteful conflict between the roles of the board (or its fund-raising committee) and the CEO (or the CEO's director of development) can be reduced, perhaps avoided, by defining the job in terms of the expected result rather than in terms of the means used to attain that result. After all, just as should be true with staff, the board's activities are not the issue, getting the job done is.

If fund-raising, public image, legislative impact, or other delegable performance areas are made board responsibilities, the board must organize to perform them. The board has the option of operating as a whole, in committees, or through individual assignments. In any event, it becomes the responsibility of the board, not staff, to develop and use whatever methods are necessary. If the board wants the staff to carry out and be responsible for the outcome of a specific task, then that task should not be part of the board's job. Policy control by the board will suffice.

Whatever the board decides about assuming more than the basic three responsibility areas, the matter must be made explicit and all further board activities made consonant. It is important that the initial three core areas, because they cannot be delegated, be given primacy. No board should add items unless it is sure its allegiance to the first three will not be diluted.

Policy Governance Is Not a "Hands-Off" Model

Because the Policy Governance approach is a radical departure from the traditional form of governance, CEOs and board members sometimes mistakenly characterize Policy Governance as a "hands-off" model of board governance. We assume that by "hands-off" they mean a laissez-faire, uninvolved approach to board control over management, wherein the board stays out of the CEO's hair. Nothing, however, could be further from the truth.

The best governance is hands off about some things and decidedly hands on about other things. The trick is in knowing when to be hands on and when to be hands off.

A responsible governing board should govern. It is not a figurehead. As owner-representative, the board holds title to the most authoritative function in the organization, a function that is more authoritative than that of its CEO, its staff professionals, its legal counsel, its auditing firm, and even its funding sources. Accompanying this considerable authority is an equally considerable accountability: the board is accountable for everything the organization is, everything it does, and everything it achieves—or fails to achieve.

The board bears the full amount of cumulative responsibility, bearing more cumulative responsibility than the CEO because the board is responsible for itself, the CEO, and the entire organization. Designing the board's job simply entails deciding what direct work the board can do to fulfill its extensive cumulative responsibility.

A Board Member's Approach to the Job

One of the reasons a board member's job is so difficult is that "the job" is essentially a group responsibility. In fact, it is hard to discuss how an individual is to approach a group task. Yet each board member has a responsibility to come with an effective mind set, to carry out his or her part of preparation and participation, and to take responsibility for the group. These are not always easy tasks.

Some advice follows on the frame of mind and individual preparations necessary for a given board member to play an effective role in creating a productive board.

1. *Be prepared to participate responsibly.* Participating responsibly means to do your homework, come prepared to work

> **Hands On!!**
>
> *Examples of What the Board Should Do Hands On*
>
> - Set the board's work plan and agenda for the year and for each meeting
> - Determine board training and development needs
> - Attend to discipline in board attendance, following bylaws and other self-imposed rules
> - Become expert in governance
> - Meet with and gather wisdom from the ownership
> - Establish the limits of the CEO's authority to budget, administer finances and compensation, establish programs, and otherwise manage the organization
> - Establish the results, recipients, and acceptable costs of those results that justify the organization's existence
> - Examine monitoring data and determine whether the CEO has used a reasonable interpretation of board-stated criteria

(sometimes the work is to listen), agree and disagree as your values dictate, and accept the group decision as legitimate even if not—in your opinion—correct. It is not acceptable, for example, to have opinions but not express them.

2. *Remember your identity is with the ownership, not the staff.* Identifying closely with your staff will be inviting in that you may be in conversation with them about issues more than you will be with the ownership. You will come to use staff's abbreviations and short-hand language. Be careful that you don't become more connected with staff than with those who own the organization. Be a microcosm of your ownership, not a shadow of the staff.

3. *Represent the ownership, not a single constituency.* You will understand and personally identify with one or more constituencies

> ☞ **Hands Off!!**
>
> *Examples of What the Board Should Keep Hands Off*
>
> - Establish services, programs, curricula, or budgets
> - Approve the CEO's personnel, program, and budgetary plans
> - Render any judgments or assessments of staff activity where no previous board expectations have been stated
> - Determine staff development needs, terminations, or promotions (except for the CEO)
> - Design staff jobs or instruct any staff member subordinate to the CEO (except when the CEO has assigned a staff member to some board function)
> - Decide on the table of organization and staffing requirements

more than others. That provincial streak is natural in everyone, but your civic trusteeship obligation is to rise above it. If you are a teacher, you are not on the board to represent teachers. If you are a private businessperson, you are not there to represent that interest. You are a board member for the broad ownership. There is no way that the board can be big enough to have a spokesperson for every legitimate interest, so in a moral sense you must stand for them all. Think of yourself as being from a constituency, but not representing it.

4. *Be responsible for group behavior and productivity.* While doing your own job as a single board member is important, it does not complete your responsibility. You must shoulder the potentially unfamiliar burden of being responsible for the group. That is, if you are part of a group that doesn't get its job done, that meddles in administration, or that breaks its own rules, you are culpable.

5. *Be a proactive board member.* You are not a board member to hear reports. You are a board member to make governance decisions. Listening while staff or committees recount what they have been busy doing is boring and unnecessary. Of course, it is sometimes important to get data through reports, but don't let that cast you in a passive role. Even when you are receiving education, do so as an active participant, searching doggedly for the wisdom that will enable good board decisions. Make "show and tell" board meetings passé.

6. *Honor divergent opinions without being intimidated by them.* You are obligated to register your honest opinion on issues the board takes up, but other board members are obligated to speak up as well. Encourage your colleagues to express their opinions without allowing your own to be submerged by louder or more insistent comrades. You are of little use to the process if full expression of your ideas can be held hostage by a louder member.

7. *Use your special expertise to inform your colleagues' wisdom.* If you work in accounting, law, construction, or another skilled field, be careful not to take your colleagues off the hook with respect to board decisions about such matters. To illustrate, an accountant board member shouldn't assume personal responsibility for assuring fiscal soundness. But it is all right for him or her to help board members understand what fiscal jeopardy looks like or what indices of fiscal health to watch carefully. With that knowledge, the board can pool its human values about risk, brinkmanship, overextension, and so forth in the creation of fiscal policies. In other words, use your special understanding to inform the board's wisdom, but never to substitute for it.

8. *Orient to the whole, not the parts.* Train yourself to examine, question, and define the big picture. Even if your expertise and comfort lie in some subpart of the organization challenge, the

subpart is not your job as a board member. You may offer your individual expertise to the CEO, should he or she wish to use it. But in such a role, accept that you are being a volunteer consultant and leave your board member hat at home.

9. *Think upward and outward more than downward and inward.* There will be great temptation to focus on what goes on with management and staff instead of what difference the organization should make in the larger world. The latter is a daunting task for which no one feels really qualified, yet it is the board member's job to tackle it.

10. *Tolerate issues that cannot be quickly settled.* Shorter-term, more concrete matters can give you a feeling of completion, but are likely to involve you in the wrong issues. If you must deal with such matters, resign from the board and apply for a staff position.

11. *Don't tolerate putting off the big issues forever.* The really big issues will often be too intimidating for you to reach a solution comfortably. Yet in most cases, the decision is being made anyway by default. Board inaction itself is a decision. Don't tolerate the making of big decisions by the timid action of not making them.

12. *Support the board's final choice.* No matter which way you voted, you are obligated to support the board's choice. This obligation doesn't mean you must pretend to agree with that choice; you may certainly maintain the integrity of your dissent even after the vote. What you must support is the legitimacy of the choice that you still don't agree with. For example, you will support without reservation that the CEO must follow the formal board decision, not yours.

13. *Don't mistake form for substance.* Don't confuse having a public relations committee with having good public relations. Don't confuse having financial reports with having sound finances. Don't confuse having a token constituent board member with

having sufficient input. Traditional governance has often defined responsible behavior procedurally (do this, review that, follow this set of steps) instead of substantively, so beware of the trap.

14. *Obsess about ends.* Keep the conversation about benefits, beneficiaries, and costs of the benefits alive at all times. Converse with staff, colleague board members, and the public about these matters. Ask questions, consider options, and otherwise fill most of your trustee consciousness with issues of ends.

15. *Don't expect agendas to be built on your interests.* The board's agenda is a product of careful crafting of the board's job, not a laundry list of trustee interests. Remember, too, that you are not on the board to help the staff with your special expertise, but to govern. No matter how well you can do a staff job, as a board member you are not there to do it or even to advise on it. If you wish to offer your help as an individual—apart from your trustee duties—do so, but take great care that all parties know you are not acting as a board member. The staff's using you as an adviser or helper must remain a staff prerogative rather than yours.

16. *The organization is not there for you.* Being an owner representative is very different from seeing the organization as your personal possession. Remember that the organization does not exist to satisfy board members' needs to feel useful, self-actualized, involved, or entertained. Of course, it's fine to feel these things and perfectly acceptable to seek whatever fulfillment governance can give you. But the board job must be designed foremost around the right of the ownership to be faithfully served in the determination of what the organization should accomplish.

17. *Squelch your individual points of view during monitoring.* Your own values count when the board is creating policies. But when the CEO's performance is monitored, you must refer

only to the criteria the board decided, not what your opinion was about those criteria. In other words, the CEO must be held accountable to the board's decisions and in fairness cannot be judged against your opinion. You should present any opinion you may have about amending the policies, of course, but not so as to contaminate the monitoring process.

18. *Support the chair in board discipline.* Although the board as a whole is responsible for its own discipline, it will have charged the chair with a special role in the group's confronting its own process. Don't make the chair's job harder, rather ask what you can do to make it easier.

Notes